A CENTURY *of*
AYLESBURY

The Market Square, viewed from the arches of the Town Hall, 1938. *(K. Vaughan)*

A CENTURY *of* AYLESBURY

KARL VAUGHAN

First published in the United Kingdom in 2002 by
Sutton Publishing Limited exclusively for
WHSmith, Greenbridge Road, Swindon SN3 3LD

British Library Cataloguing in Publication Data
A catalogue record for this book is available from the British Library.

ISBN 0-7509-3102-7

Illustrations

Front endpaper: Aerial view of Aylesbury, 1927.
Back endpaper: Aerial view of Aylesbury, 1998.
Half title page: Mence Smith hardware store, Cambridge Street, 1950.
Title page: Stoke Road, *c.* 1900.

Typeset in 11/14pt Photina and produced by
Sutton Publishing Limited, Phoenix Mill,
Thrupp, Stroud, Gloucestershire GL5 2BU.
Printed and bound in England by
J.H. Haynes & Co. Ltd, Sparkford.

Contents

A view of Temple Square looking towards Church Street, mid-1950s. On the right is the Queen's Head pub. *(M. Sale)*

Introduction

A hundred years ago Aylesbury was a busy market town with lots of people coming here to trade and to buy and sell livestock. Although technology has changed over the years, Aylesbury is still a busy market town. To keep up with the latest trends, various areas of the town have been demolished and rebuilt. Many shops have come and gone and the town has expanded to keep pace with the population increase. With this influx of people from other towns and countries the Aylesbury accent and dialect has virtually disappeared. It is largely spoken by people over 50 who were born and bred in the town, and is a rare treat to hear.

So, what is *A Century of Aylesbury* all about? Well, the idea was suggested to me by the publishers of this book. I had to get together a collection of photographs that reflect the changing face of Aylesbury in the twentieth century. This was by no means simple. At first I thought about how I was to approach this task. The early part of the century is

Army manoeuvres on the outskirts of Aylesbury around the time of the First World War. *(R.J. Johnson)*

Looking up the High Street, early 1920s. The turning for Exchange Street is on the left. *(M. Sale)*

fairly easy to feature as there are many different postcards to choose from. A particularly good photograph I have used is of the teachers and pupils of Temple School, Buckingham Street, in 1921. I found this at a postcard fair a year or two ago. The Second World War period was particularly challenging until I discovered some photographs of the aftermath of the Walton landmine explosion of 1940. These came from the Hazell's collection which is deposited in the Record Office. I am pleased to be able to use these photographs in this book, as they have never been published before and they show just what a dramatic and destructive event this was. Postcards again have been used for the 1950s, which show a busy town with lots of traffic about. This takes us to the 1960s where I have used photographs that I wasn't able to use in my previous book, *Aylesbury in the 1960s*. Some of these show how the town was torn apart by the developers. The 1970s saw one of the greatest things ever to happen to Aylesbury – Friars Club. The club ran from 1969 to 1984 and saw artists such as David Bowie, Lou Reed, Genesis, The Jam, Blondie, Roxy Music and Black Sabbath, as well as many others, appearing live on stage. The former owner, David Stopps, has very kindly lent me some material to include in this book. In the 1980s little happened to the town. In the 1990s Friars Square underwent a much-needed facelift bringing it more up to date. And arriving at the new millennium I wondered

A bus coming into town on Buckingham Street, 1965. On the right, construction of Heron House is nearing completion. *(D. Bailey)*

whether Aylesbury has really changed that much. OK, we've seen an increase in the size of the town, we've got more roads to drive on, more houses to live in, but the feel of the town seems much the same. It seems that some people expect Aylesbury to be a fast-paced town but it has always been a rather laid-back place.

Because of the limited number of photographs I have been able to include in this book, I am unable to feature every event that has occurred in the last century. So it is not meant to be a complete chronicle of the twentieth century. This would take a very long time to complete, and as six months was the timescale given to complete this book I was unable to spend time sourcing particular photographs, like the coronation of Queen Elizabeth II for instance. Despite limitations such as these, I hope that you feel this book has turned out well and are pleased with the variety and quality of photographs used. I hope you enjoy this little journey through the twentieth century as much as I have done. Maybe I'll do it again some time.

Karl Vaughan
Aylesbury, 2002

The Dark Lantern pub in Silver Street, early 1950s. The building with the bicycle leaning against it is Jones & Cocks, ironmongers. *(R.J. Johnson)*

*The First
Twenty Years*

A view of the Market Square, *c.* 1905. *(K. Vaughan)*

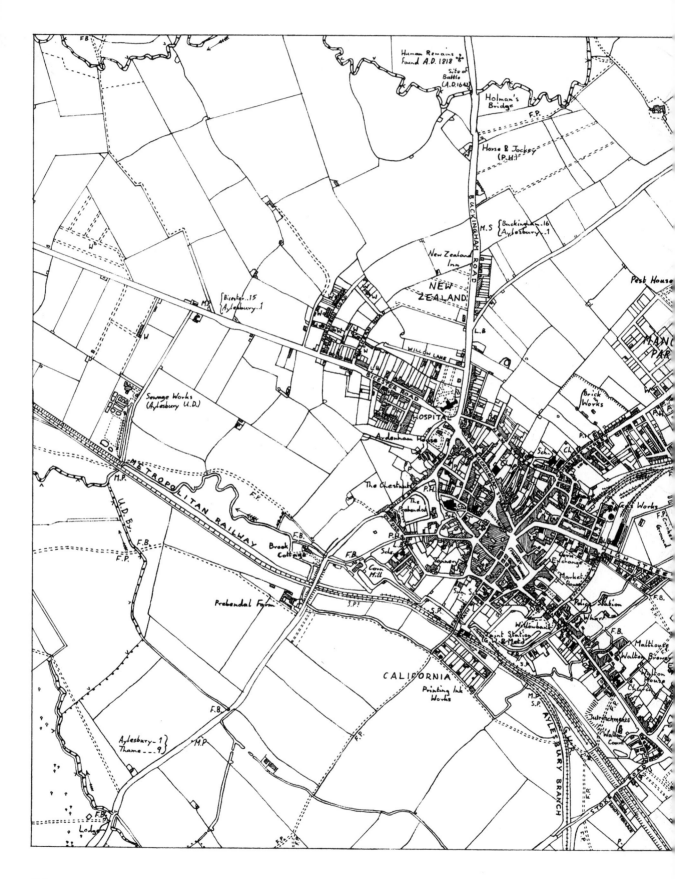

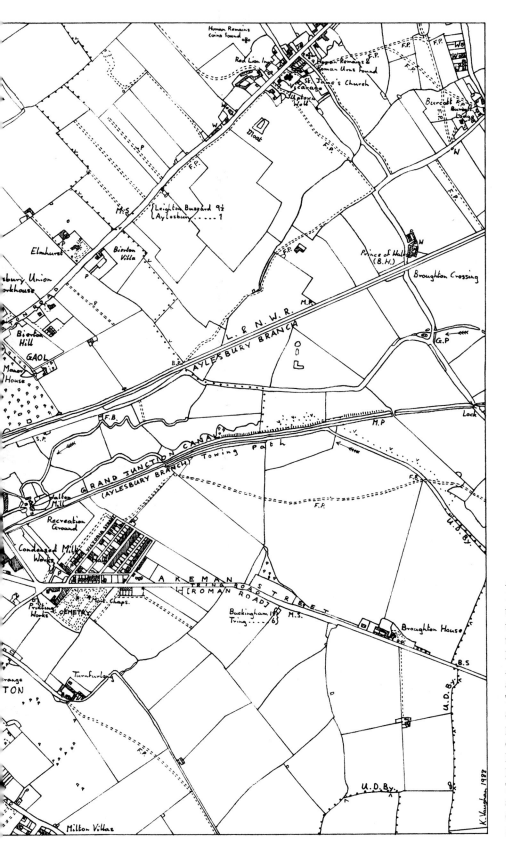

A map of the town in 1900. This shows clearly the amount of land that was still undeveloped on the outskirts of the town. Many of the inhabitants of Aylesbury were living above their places of work. There were many slum areas in the town too, in particular Spring Gardens off White Hill, Upper Hundreds and Prospect Place off Walton Street. The LNWR branch railway stretches off towards Cheddington on the right. (K. Vaughan)

Tring Road, *c.* 1900. On the left is the cemetery, which was opened in 1857. Further down the road is the large factory of printers Hazell, Watson & Viney. *(M. Sale)*

A view down Walton Street, *c.* 1900. This is a scene which is instantly recognizable. All of the buildings on the right still remain. Behind the hedge next to which the man carrying a case is walking was Walton Court Farm. Round the back of the farm was a field known by locals as 'Humpy Bumpy Field' because it was very undulating. *(M. Sale)*

The Grand Union Canal looking towards town, *c.* 1900. On the right are houses fronting Park Street. On the horizon between the trees St Mary's Church can be seen. *(M. Sale)*

Walton Road, *c.* 1900. The large barn on the right belonged to Walton Grange. Most of the houses seen in this photograph were destroyed by the landmine explosion of 1940, which is illustrated in a later chapter. *(M. Sale)*

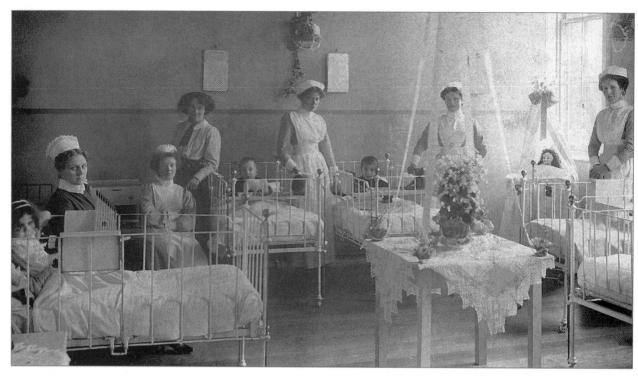

The children's ward of the Buckinghamshire Infirmary, Buckingham Road, *c.* 1900. The hospital was formed in 1832 using an older building on the same site called Dawney's Nursery. It was rebuilt forty years later and is now known as the Royal Buckinghamshire Hospital. *(R.J. Johnson)*

A view of Kingsbury, *c.* 1900. This part of town was originally the site of the ancient manor house for the lords of Aylesbury. Some people call this area Kingsbury Square, which is slightly misleading: although it is an open area it is actually triangular in shape. *(M. Sale)*

Bicester Road, *c.* 1900. In the centre just behind the horse and cart is the Hop Pole Inn which stands on the corner of Southern Road. Beyond these houses were mainly fields and the road was little more than a dirt track. The turning on the immediate left is Townsend Piece. *(M. Sale)*

Walton Pond, *c.* 1900. In those days Walton was still regarded as a separate part of the town. It was originally a hamlet on the outskirts of Aylesbury but was eventually encompassed by the ever-growing town. The buildings facing us in the distance are on Wendover Road. *(R.J. Johnson)*

Looking along Stoke Road on a quiet day, *c.* 1900. This is a delightful period photograph showing the local inhabitants along with the newly built houses which still front this road. In the distance can be seen the Old Stoke Road going off over the railway bridge into the countryside – there was no Southcourt in those days. Also of note is the rather elaborate sign-writing on the shopfront of the Mandeville Tobacco & Confectionery Stores. Given how busy this road is today, it is unlikely that one would be able readily to take a photograph from the same spot. *(K. Vaughan)*

Bourbon Street, *c.* 1900. At the end of the street is a horse and cart waiting outside the grocer and wine merchant, Miles Thomas Cocks. This was here until 1964 when, along with all of the buildings on that side of the road, it was demolished to make way for Friars Square. *(D. Bailey)*

The Bell Hotel decorated for the coronation of King Edward VII in 1902. This is a building which has undergone many alterations over the centuries. It is thought to date from the sixteenth century and probably started life as a tavern. Its façade in this picture appears to be of around 1830. Since then, of course, it has been altered once again, with a new floor being added together with a bay window to the left of the main entrance. *(M. Sale)*

A view of the carnage after the infamous rail disaster at Aylesbury Town station on 23 December 1904. A newspaper train from London left the rails at about 4.30 a.m., while travelling at a speed which was reputed to be 60 miles per hour. It then ploughed on to the neighbouring rails. A parcel train coming from the opposite direction tore into the wreckage, demolishing some of the south end of the platform and bringing down a signal with it. Four men were killed and several injured in the accident. *(M. Sale)*

Apart from the fact that the train was going too fast, the turn into the station was too tight, and this caused the train to lose control. After the accident, work began on making the turn less dangerous. *(D. Bailey)*

A quaint view of the High Street, *c.* 1905. Almost eighty years since this road was built there were still many properties that were private residences, with walls and railings fronting the street. Seen clearly right of centre is Longley's the draper, a well-established firm in the town. *(K. Vaughan)*

Cambridge Street, *c.* 1905. An interesting part of this view is in the centre beyond the group of men. It shows the buildings that were there before the original Odeon cinema was built. On the left is the rear entrance to Ye Olde Harrow Inn, the main entrance being in Buckingham Street. *(K. Vaughan)*

Church Street, 1907. Back in the early nineteenth century this was known as Broad Street, most likely because it was, and indeed still is, wider than most of the roads in this area. Just behind the trees is St Mary's Church. *(K. Vaughan)*

The teachers and pupils of the Grammar School, 1907. This was taken at their new premises on Walton Road, which opened in 1906. The school was originally in Church Street – the old building is now home to the Buckinghamshire County Museum. *(R.J. Johnson)*

A picturesque view of the Market Square covered by snow, 26 April 1908. This freak of weather prompted a few of the town's photographers to get their cameras out. *(R. Adams)*

28

An advert for Dukes china shop in Market Street, *c.* 1908. *(R.J. Johnson)*

A rather deserted view of Market Square, *c.* 1908. It is quite unusual to see the square like this as it is normally a very busy place. *(K. Vaughan)*

Market Square, *c.* 1908. This is a view of the square before both the John Hampden and Lord Beaconsfield statues were put in. Just beyond the lamp-post on the right is the Crown Hotel, which had just had its name painted on to the bare brickwork in the typical style of those times. *(K. Vaughan)*

Queens Park, *c.* 1910. This view is from Princes Road looking towards the High Street. To the right is the entrance to Queens Park Road and further down is the Kings Road entrance. Baldwin's sweet shop on the left proved very popular with the schoolchildren of Queens Park School for many years. *(R.J. Johnson)*

Turnfurlong viewed from the end of Highbridge Road, *c.* 1910. This was just a narrow lane leading to Turnfurlong Farm and eventually Bedgrove Farm. Behind the gate to the right are the grounds of Walton Grange. The porch in the foreground formed part of the Millwrights Arms pub. *(R.J. Johnson)*

This charming photograph from about 1910 shows a house on the corner of Fleet Street and New Street. It was the home of the Luff family who, as is indicated by the sign on the building, were coal merchants. (*R.J. Johnson*)

Walton Street, 1910. This view is looking towards town and shows the familiar row of buildings on the right which look remarkably unchanged today. Behind the large tree in the centre is Walton Church. The painted building on the left advertises Longley's drapers, which was in the High Street. *(R.J. Johnson)*

The Manor Park estate, *c.* 1910. These photographs were taken not long after the estate was largely completed. The houses on Vale Road would have had a clear view towards the north-west as there were no houses on the opposite side of the road at that time. *(K. Vaughan)*

Market Square, *c.* 1910. This photograph was taken before the statue of Lord Chesham was placed between the two lions. These lions stood in the grounds of Waddesdon Manor before being given to the town by Baron Ferdinand de Rothschild. They were brought by steam roller from there in January 1888. *(K. Vaughan)*

Looking down Princes Road on the Queens Park estate, *c.* 1910. Houses in Highbridge Road are seen facing us with Beaconsfield Road beyond. *(R.J. Johnson)*

Highbridge Road looking towards town, *c.* 1910. As with
Manor Park, these houses too were newly built and appear
quite uniform with their neat brick walls and railings.
(R.J. Johnson)

Holy Trinity Church on Walton Street, *c.* 1910. The church
was built in 1845 and enlarged in 1886–7. To the right of
the church is Croft Passage. *(K. Vaughan)*

The statue of John Hampden in Market Square, 1912. The foundation stone was laid on 22 June 1911 which was the coronation day of King George V. The statue was sculpted by H.C. Fehr and was unveiled on 27 June 1912. Both the statue and bas-reliefs of 'The Battle of Chalgrove Field' and 'The Burial of John Hampden' were presented as a coronation gift to the county by James Griffin of Long Marston. The statue has recently been moved to a different site at the top of the High Street, just a few yards away. *(K. Vaughan)*

Walton Engine Works, 1912. The works were situated in Walton Road opposite the grounds of Walton Grange. Run by William Morris, they produced ironwork among other things. Some of it is still in existence to this day: dotted around the town are some of their road drain covers. *(R.J. Johnson)*

The High Street, 1914. The post office seen here was opened on 25 November 1889. This building was originally home to the Telephone Exchange before the new one opened in New Street on 8 March 1957. *(K. Vaughan)*

Army manoeuvres on the outskirts of Aylesbury around the time of the First World War. I was recently talking to someone who remembers these manoeuvres going on down Turnfurlong. The men would charge with their bayonets at bags of straw hanging from a goalpost-like structure. *(R.J. Johnson)*

Looking towards Buckingham Road from the end of Buckingham Street, *c.* 1915. The Royal Buckinghamshire Hospital is on the left. The two buildings on the right are Melrose House, nearest, and the Primitive Methodist church which opened in 1882. The last service held there was in March 1951. Both buildings have since been demolished. *(R. Adams)*

Walton Pond, 1915. The cows seen here are probably on their way to the market in town. On the left are the Victorian houses that were destroyed by the landmine of 1940. Views of this destruction are seen later in this book. *(R.J. Johnson)*

Buckingham Street, 1916. Instantly recognizable is the large Methodist chapel down the street. Just up the street towards us is a jumble of items for sale outside Jenns, the house furnishers. The next shop along is the draper's shop of Frank Madder. *(K. Vaughan)*

Market Square, 1917. To the right of the picture a busy sheep market is in progress. The selling of livestock in the square ceased in 1927 when the new cattle market was opened behind the Town Hall, which is the large building with the arches at the far end of the square. *(R.J. Johnson)*

Market Street, 1918. The gable-fronted building on the left is Duke's china shop. I have recently been told by Mr George Adams, who is in his nineties, that as a young man when he was in the shop with a raincoat on, he turned round and caused a display of wares to come crashing down. *(R. Adams)*

The
1920s and 1930s

The Crown Hotel at the top of the High Street, 1920s. *(M. Sale)*

We open this chapter with a photograph of the teachers and pupils of Temple School in Buckingham Street, February 1920. The school started in Temple Square in the late 1880s and was run by Miss Locke. who came from a well-known Aylesbury family. At the turn of the twentieth century it was taken over by Miss Amery and Miss Gleaves, and continued on that site for a few years until about 1910 when they moved to Putnam House in Buckingham Street. The house was used for

boarders, while at the rear were classrooms that backed on to New Street. This was where the Upper School was situated. In Church Street was Temple School's kindergarten. In about 1936 we find that Putnam House has become the home of the Mid-Bucks Shelter & Maternity Home, but the school was still there behind it. By 1940 the school had disappeared, both from Buckingham Street and Church Street. Putnam House itself was demolished in 1970. *(K. Vaughan)*

A 30-ton German tank in the High Street on 24 March 1920. It was captured during the First World War and given to the town by the National War Savings Committee. Its destination was Kingsbury and it remained there for nine years. In June 1929 there was an explosion when two men were using blow-torches to dismantle the tank. One of the workers was thrown 6 feet into the air and a distance of 20 yards. The other, who was on top of the tank, caught the full force of the blast and was thrown to the ground with his clothes alight. The blast was thought to have been caused by a concealed petrol tank deep inside the machine. It was reported that the explosion threw one of the worker's hammers into a garden in Kingsbury. A chisel was found in a neighbouring yard. *(R. Adams)*

Walton Street, *c.* 1920. Behind the houses on the left were some of the poorer parts of town, namely Prospect Place and Garner's Row. They were demolished in around 1925. In the years following, all of the buildings on that side would also be demolished. *(M. Sale)*

Market Square, 1921. The war memorial seen here had just been built. Beyond it is the George Hotel, which was closed in that year. Just visible on the far right is scaffolding surrounding Lloyd's Bank which was undergoing expansion at the time. *(K. Vaughan)*

Station Street, *c.* 1921. Here we see a large group of people posing for a photograph just before going off on an outing. They are outside the original Prince of Wales pub, which was later rebuilt to a different design. Further up the street on the far right of the picture is the yard of builders Mayne & Son. *(R.J. Johnson)*

45

Kingsbury, 1921. The tank featured on page 44 is seen in its final resting place. The fountain in front of it was later moved to its present position in Vale Park. Behind it to the left is the shop of basketmaker Amos Charles Fleet. The Rockwood pub is to the left: at this time it was smaller than it is today. *(R.J. Johnson)*

Market Square, *c.* 1922. At the top of the square the large sign of the George Hotel has been removed because of its closure. The building was taken over by the Territorial Association in 1921, and it was demolished in 1935 when Burtons menswear built their shop on the site. *(K. Vaughan)*

The printing works of Hazell, Watson & Viney on the Tring Road, early 1920s. Here we see some of the firm's delivery vehicles. *(R.J. Johnson)*

Walton Way, early 1920s. Taken from Tring Road, this shows the houses that were built for workers at the nearby factory of Hazell, Watson & Viney. *(R.J. Johnson)*

The war memorial of Hazell, Watson & Viney on the corner of the High Street and Walton Road, early 1920s. The memorial was erected in memory of sixty-five employees who lost their lives during the First World War. It was unveiled by the Marquess of Lincolnshire on 20 November 1920. A tablet with seventeen names was added after the Second World War. Sadly this memorial no longer exists, as a roundabout was put here in the late 1960s. *(R.J. Johnson)*

Hartwell Road, *c.* 1925. This is a view of the road just before it turns at the Bugle Horn pub, and what a peaceful scene this is. It is quite different today – a very busy main road into Aylesbury. *(R.J. Johnson)*

Members of the Dramatic Society of Hazell, Watson & Viney parading in the Market Square, mid-1920s. *(R.J. Johnson)*

Market Square, late 1920s. The Bull's Head Hotel in the left background had just recently been refronted by its proprietor G. Gargini. The large Victorian building in the centre is the Westminster Bank. Two doors down from there is Armstrong's stationers – one of quite a few places in the town where one could buy picture postcards of Aylesbury and the surrounding area. *(K. Vaughan)*

Another busy Market Square scene, late 1920s. Even by this time the town centre was getting increasingly busier with motor vehicles. It wouldn't be long before town planners were thinking of ways to ease the flow of traffic. Many of the schemes dreamt up in the 1920s and '30s were not implemented until after the Second World War. *(K. Vaughan)*

Cattle Market, *c.* 1930. The large building at the back is the Town Hall. Adjoining it was the premises of T. Loader, corn merchant. *(R.J. Johnson)*

A bus in Kingsbury. *c.* 1930. The bus station was established here in 1929. This photograph was taken some time before the shelter was built in 1938. The Kingsbury Café seen on the left behind the bus was an ideal place to pass time while waiting for a bus. *(D. Bailey)*

Another view of Kingsbury at about the same time. This clearly shows the Aylesbury Motor Company on the right advertising the many different makes of cars that they sold – Sunbeam, Triumph, Morris, Hillman, Fiat, Singer, Riley and Austin. Quite a selection! *(R.J. Johnson)*

A sunny Market Square, 1933. Up on the left past Jones & Cocks is the Old Beams Restaurant, which is seen again later on in this chapter. Just visible at the top of the square in Kingsbury is Bradford's, the ironmongers. Their premises were demolished in 1934 to make the turning easier for vehicles coming out of Buckingham Street. Brooke House now stands on the site. *(K. Vaughan)*

Market Square, 1933. This shows the Crown Hotel after it had been refurbished in the same year. It is a great shame that this turned out to be in vain, as it was demolished in 1937 to have shops built on its site. *(K. Vaughan)*

Castle Street, mid-1930s. This street shares a characteristic with Walton Road and Walton Street: they have all had their surfaces lowered to make travelling easier for horses coming into town with carts. At the end of the street the pub sign for the Black Horse can be seen. This pub closed in around 1938. *(M. Sale)*

Market Square. The procession seen here was for the Royal Bucks Hospital Extension Appeal Week and shows an old-time stage coach on its way through the square. The appeal was held in July 1935 and 1936, and other events included a swimming gala at the Vale Pool, a masked ball at the Town Hall and decorated vehicles that proceeded through the town. *(R.J. Johnson)*

Market Square decorated for the coronation of King George VI, 1937. *(D. Bailey)*

This is how Walton Street looked during the coronation. These two photographs must have been taken on a Sunday judging by how deserted the town looks. *(D. Bailey)*

Old Beams Restaurant, Market Square, 1938. This was one of the oldest buildings in the square and was tucked away behind Jones & Cocks, ironmongers. *(R.J. Johnson)*

A view of the interior of the restaurant, showing how quaint it was. This building together with its neighbours was demolished in 1964 to make way for Friars Square. *(R.J. Johnson)*

Vale Park. 1938. Formerly the meeting-place of the Vale of Aylesbury Cycling and Athletic Club, the ground was bought by the Corporation in 1929. Tennis courts were opened in the same year and on 1 July 1937 the park itself was opened by Alderman A.T. Adkins, who was the mayor at that time. *(R. Adams)*

Church Street, 1939. This view shows the very fine frontage of the Chantry on the immediate left, which is a sixteenth-century building altered in the 1840s. In the 1860s it was the home of Robert Gibbs, who wrote his *History of Aylesbury*. This was published in 1885 and is still a very interesting read today. *(K. Vaughan)*

The Gaol on Bierton Road, late 1930s. The building opened in 1847 having moved from Market Square. Public executions continued at the new gaol: over the main archway was a drop mechanism for hangings. On 24 March 1854 the first execution at the drop was of a man called Moses Hatto, who committed murder at Burnham Abbey. The last public execution held here was in 1864. *(K. Vaughan)*

Parsons Fee, late 1930s. This narrow lane connects Castle Street with Church Street. In the foreground is the memorial commemorating the First World War. It was unveiled by the Marquess of Lincolnshire on 20 March 1925. Being in a conservation area, Parsons Fee still retains its character. *(K. Vaughan)*

The Pavilion in the High Street, 1939. The cinema was built on a former builder's yard and was opened on 2 March 1925. It was then enlarged in 1936 and remained the Pavilion up until June 1947, when it was renamed as the Granada. (*R. Adams*)

Through the War Years
and on to the 1950s

Victorian houses damaged by the Walton landmine explosion, 1940. *(E. Viney)*

Market Square, 1940. In the distance is the entrance to Great Western Street, with the Greyhound pub standing at the bottom of Silver Street. *(R.J. Johnson)*

On 25 September 1940 a landmine exploded in Walton Road behind Walton Grange. People nearby saw something float down from the enemy aircraft in a sort of parachute. When it went off the explosion was beyond belief. In this photograph we see workers sifting through debris in the crater which was left by the blast. The building behind is Walton Grange: the damage to this fifteenth-century building was so severe that it was demolished shortly afterwards: a great shame. *(E. Viney)*

Other buildings which suffered badly from the explosion were those fronting Walton Pond. These were solidly built Victorian houses. Mr J. Johnson, who lived lived at 20 Walton Road, was killed when the landmine went off. It was rumoured that he was looking for his cat at the time. In the distance are houses on Walton Road which still exist today. Being further away, they suffered only superficial damage. *(E. Viney)*

These cottages on the opposite side of the road to Walton Grange were also severely damaged. They were of a similar age to the Grange. Being timber framed they must have just shaken to bits. *(E. Viney)*

A final look at the Walton landmine damage. Here we see a view down Walton Road taken from near its junction with Wendover Road. This really does show how much mess was made by the explosion – the force of the blast must have been incredible. Even a few buildings in town suffered with blown out windows. It's a wonder that the houses on the left weren't more severely damaged. (E. Viney)

Walton Street, 1941. On the left are the original county offices, opened in 1929. The railings disappeared soon after this photograph was taken. *(R. Adams)*

Walton Road, 1947. A more tranquil view of this area after the damage shown earlier in this chapter. All of the repair work to these houses had been finished for some time, with virtually all of the glass from their windows being replaced. The pond looks clear compared with its condition today – lots of plants have been allowed to grow there now. *(R.J. Johnson)*

An advert for Spragg's in the High Street, 1947. *(K. Vaughan)*

Market Square,
c. 1948. On the right
is the clothing store of
William McIlroy,
which was rebuilt in
1954 when Courts
moved in. *(M. Sale)*

Cambridge Street, April 1950. Next to the hardware shop of Mence Smith is Millburn's Auction Rooms. The building was erected in 1881 and the upper floor was leased from 1907 to Valentine Jarvis, draper, in the High Street. After the auction rooms closed in 1950 the whole building was occupied by Jarvis until 1981, when it was demolished. *(J. Millburn)*

Eagles Road, early 1950s. The road at that time was more like a dirt track. On the left behind the fence is the sports ground of Hazell, Watson & Viney. *(R.J. Johnson)*

The Oddfellows Arms on a wet day in the early 1950s. The man on the left is a postman on his way back to the depot at Upper Hundreds, which is just round the corner on the left. *(R.J. Johnson)*

A display in the shop window of Sale Brothers, grocers, in Buckingham Street, in the early 1950s. *(M. Sale)*

Looking up Park Street, early 1950s. At the very top of the street are buildings fronting Cambridge Street. On the right are the signal-box and gates at the level crossing. This was part of the LMS line which went from Aylesbury to Cheddington and had its station in the High Street. Photographs of the station may be seen later in this book. (R.J. Johnson)

St Mary's Square after a good fall of snow, early 1950s. Just to the left of the white cottages is the Evangelist Hall, which was built in 1878. It was demolished and rebuilt in the 1960s. (R.J. Johnson)

Temple Street from Temple Square, *c*. 1954. This is a part of town that hasn't altered much over the years. The Queen's Head on the left is still one of Aylesbury's more traditional pubs. *(M. Sale)*

High Street, 1955. This is viewed from the entrance to Britannia Street, which is on the left. Earlier in this book we saw a photograph of the Pavilion cinema. Here we see it renamed the Granada. On the left is one of Ivatt's shoe shops, the other being in Kingsbury. *(M. Sale)*

The Benjamin Disraeli statue in Market Square, mid-1950s. To the left is the side entrance to the Bull's Head Hotel. This passage is one of the oldest in the town today; however, the hotel itself has since gone. *(R.J. Johnson)*

A busy bus station in Kingsbury, mid-1950s. On the left is Loader's, the corn and seed merchants, who had their stores at the rear of the Town Hall in Market Square. *(R.J. Johnson)*

Temple Square, mid-1950s. This view shows the premises of builders Gilkes & Son at the top of Castle Street. The pub sign on the right is that of the Queen's Head. *(R.J. Johnson)*

Buses in Kingsbury, mid-1950s. In the distance on the right we can see buildings in George Street. On the corner for some years was a rose garden that occupied the site of a demolished building until about 1959, when Kingsbury House was built there. Just visible is the row of cottages that used to front George Street. They were to the left of the entrance to the King's Head and were demolished shortly after this photograph was taken. *(D. Bailey)*

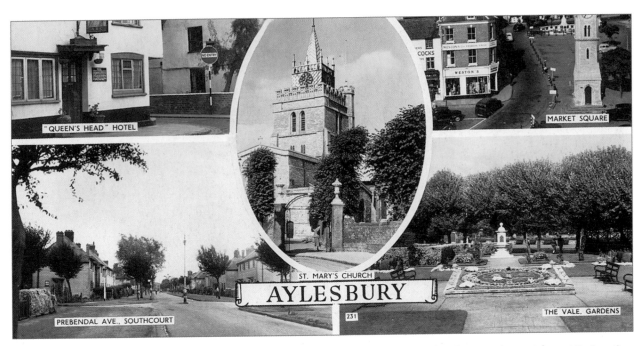

The bottom left view in this composite postcard shows Prebendal Avenue, *c.* 1957. The photograph was taken at its junction with Hampden Road and looks towards Chestnut Crescent at the very end. Note the size of the grass verges – they have since been reduced to make the road wider for traffic. The Southcourt estate was started in 1920 and people were moved there from the slum areas of the town that were being demolished at the time. Prospect Place, Upper Hundreds and Whitehall Row were some of the areas that were cleared. *(K. Vaughan)*

High Street. 1958. On the left is the tall frontage of the Granada cinema. Opposite there is Clarke's china shop with the clothes shop of George Tough next door. *(M. Sale)*

Walton Street looking towards town, 1958. The original County Offices are seen on the right. Facing them in the foreground is the Old House, a large building that disappeared for the construction of the new County Offices and library. Next door to it up the street was Walton Cottage, which also disappeared in the redevelopment. *(M. Sale)*

A busy High Street, 1958. On the left is drapers Spragg & Son. The large building further down is Crown Buildings, which takes its name from the Crown Hotel that was there before. Immediately on the right is the National Provincial Bank. *(M. Sale)*

Market Square, 1958. Jones & Cocks, ironmongers (centre left), was demolished in 1962 when Freeman, Hardy & Willis built an extension to their shoe shop on the site. The shop was round the corner from Westons. (*M. Sale*)

A bus going through the very narrow junction at the top of Buckingham Street, 1959. As more and more traffic went through town, this junction was one of the first to be altered: a pub called the Plough was demolished to allow road widening to take place. Behind the bus is the depot of the St John Ambulance Brigade. (*D. Bailey*)

High Street Station, *c.* 1959. This photograph is taken from the sidings of coal merchant William Hawkins. The station itself was closed to passengers on 31 January 1953 and was demolished in 1960. The track remained for a couple of years until it was taken up. *(D. Bailey)*

A view along the platform of High Street station, *c.* 1959. Here we can see some goods wagons. Today it is hard to visualize all of this: it is now a shopping area called Vale Park Drive. *(D. Bailey)*

The 1960s and 1970s

Walton Street, 1960. *(M. Sale)*

Two Brewers Yard, Buckingham Street, 1960. Originally this yard would have been the stables for the inn. Here we see it used as a car park. On the left is the white wall of the Two Brewers. The wall stretching down on the right is the rear of Baker's cycle and toy shop. *(M. Sale)*

A view of the canal from the footbridge at Highbridge Walk, 1962. Straight ahead is the flour mill of Hills & Partridge, while to the right of that is the chimney of the Nestlé factory. *(M. Sale)*

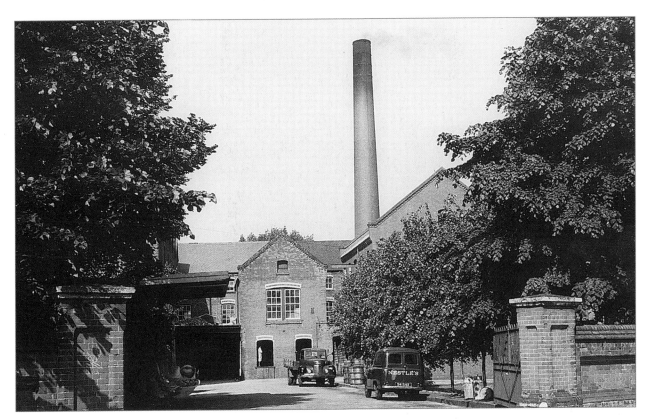

One of Nestlé's yards from the High Street, 1962. This photograph was taken before much of the old factory was demolished and a new block was constructed in its place. *(M. Sale)*

Deep snow during the long cold winter of 1962/3. This was taken from the garden of my grandparents' house at 157 Buckingham Road, and is typical of the scene all over the town at that time. The canal was frozen over for months and plenty of garden vegetables were ruined. *(K. Vaughan)*

Market Square, 1963. To the right the Clock Tower can just be seen. Behind it is the shoe shop of Freeman, Hardy & Willis. The buildings facing us on the left disappeared in the following year to make way for Friars Square shopping centre. *(M. Sale)*

Walton Road, 1963. This view is from the Wendover Road end and presents a rather tranquil scene compared to twenty-three years previously when the landmine went off nearby. Walton Road still looks much the same today, although the terracing stops at the end of the large house up on the left where a small road has been put through for access to some flats. *(M. Sale)*

Market Square, 1963. This is from the entrance of Walton Street and shows on the left the clothes shop of Weaver to Wearer, a building that in a year would be levelled to make way for Friars Square. The building on the immediate right with the Trust House sign is the Bell Hotel. *(K. Vaughan)*

The yard of Walton Brewery, 1963. The brewery occupied a large area on Walton Street for many years and at that time was owned by Aylesbury Brewery Company. In 1965 everything was demolished and replaced by a new building at the rear of the site. At the front Planar Precinct was built, a long, large 1960s building. Now it too has been demolished and has partly been replaced by a modern office block. This ever-changing town! *(M. Sale)*

Looking up Walton Street at its junction with Exchange Street, 1963. This was taken during the first stages of demolition of Walton Cottage, which is the large white building in the centre. On its site the new library and County Offices were built. *(M. Sale)*

Houses in Exchange Street, 1963. Where the people are crossing was the yard of the Chandos Hotel, which stood at the end of the street. That building together with these houses disappeared in 1981, to be replaced by a large office block called 66 The Exchange. *(M. Sale)*

This is a good view of the town in 1963, from the rear of the old County Offices on Walton Street. The cattle market and Exchange Street are below. The large square building on the horizon is the newly built extension to the Nestlé factory on the High Street. *(R. Adams)*

Market Square, 1964. This shows the row of buildings that was soon to be demolished for the construction of Friars Square. Old Beams Restaurant is straight ahead. At the right of the building is a passage that led to the rear of the Dark Lantern pub. (M. Sale)

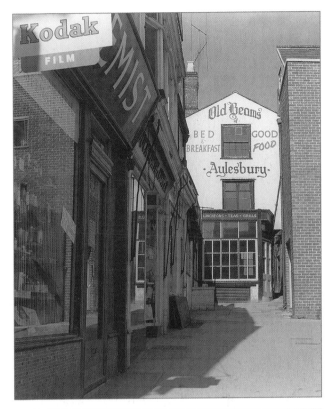

Looking down Bourbon Street, 1964. The white building on the right was for many years the offices of the *Bucks Advertiser* newspaper. Next door to it is the Tinder Box café. In the latter part of 1964 all of the buildings on that side of the road were torn down to make way for Friars Square. (M. Sale)

The demolition of Silver Street, 1964. This was part of the scheme to redevelop the town centre and create a new shopping area, together with car parks and bigger roads, to better serve Aylesbury's increasing population. (*M. Sale*)

The last remains of some of the buildings in Market Square. When cleared, this area would form part of the entrance to Friars Square. Note the plaque on the wall of the Coach & Horses on the far left. This was the sign for ABC Ales (the Aylesbury Brewery Co.): they were made of solid slate with inset gold lettering and covered with glass about 5 mm thick. They would be very decorative collectors' items today. (*M. Sale*)

Turnfurlong, 1964. A dead give-away for the period is the car parked on the right – a three-wheeled bubble car, popular in the 1950s and '60s. The road has been made up and now leads to the Bedgrove Estate, which was then in its infancy. *(M. Sale)*

Loader's corn merchant's building at the rear of the Town Hall, 1964. Beyond it is the cattle market, with buildings in Exchange Street facing us at the very bottom. A more recent view of this area is seen on page 122. *(M. Sale)*

A rather quiet view of Walton Street, 1964. Normally this would be a very busy road, even in those days. This photograph was taken from outside the Ship Inn. Walton Baptist church was at this time being stripped in preparation for its demolition. *(M. Sale)*

Looking up Walton Street from the forecourt of Claude Rye's garage, 1964. This gives a good view of the buildings of the Aylesbury Brewery Company on the left. A little further up the road the tower of Holy Trinity Church can be seen. *(M. Sale)*

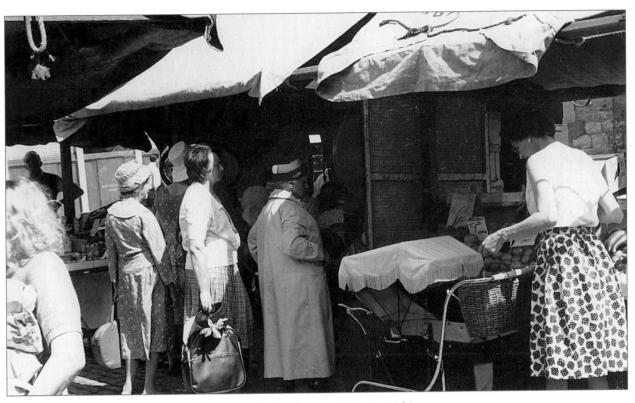

People doing their shopping on market day in the Market Square, 1964. *(M. Sale)*

A busy Kingsbury scene, 1964. Visible here in the background on the left is the Eagle pub, which closed in 1975. It was one of the town's smallest pubs. The building still survives today and is used as a restaurant. *(D. Bailey)*

Beaconsfield Road, 1965. This photograph was taken from the Highbridge Road end and shows building work going on for the construction of the new Aylesbury Brewery Company buildings. The buildings just past the Victorian houses on the left were part of the Technical College. *(M. Sale)*

Buckingham Street, 1965. A good contrast of old and new here as we see the newly built Heron House office block dwarfing everything else around it. Harper's monumental mason's yard and the row of white buildings seen here soon disappeared to become a car park. *(M. Sale)*

A carnival procession in the High Street during the Borough Council's Golden Jubilee celebrations, 1966. Other events included a cycle race and a concert in the Market Square. *(M. Sale)*

Walton Street looking towards town, 1967. The building on the immediate right was home to the Copper Kettle café. Opposite it is the entrance to Brook Street. All the buildings between the Copper Kettle and the old police garages at the end would soon be gone, to be replaced by a roundabout. *(M. Sale)*

Stalls in the cattle market, 1967. The Market Square can just be seen through the arches at the top. As is shown later on, the cattle market area has been replaced by a cinema complex. *(M. Sale)*

Friars Square, 1968. This is how the shopping centre looked shortly after opening. At this time the Woolworths side had not yet been completed. The market had moved from the Market Square to the sunken area at the top of this slope, just below the cafeteria which is shown looming on the horizon. *(R.J. Johnson)*

FRIARS AYLESBURY
Summer 1971

Sat. June 12	FLEETWOOD MAC and Gothic Horizon	60P
-- -- 19	GENESIS and Chameleon	50P
-- -- 26	PINK FAIRIES	50P
Fri. July 2	THE FACES and a surprise...	£1★
Sat. -- 10	VAN DER GRAAF GENERATOR and...?	50P
-- -- 17	ATOMIC ROOSTER and something else!	70P
-- -- 24	an evening with QUINTESSENCE	70P
-- -- 31	EAST OF EDEN and Home	
-- Aug. 7		
-- -- 14	RORY GALLAGHER	
-- -- 21	QUIVER	
-- -- 28	OSIBISA	
-- Sep. 4	MOTT the HOOPLE	
-- -- 11	EDGAR BROUGHTON	

★ (tickets available in advance)

Some of the bands appearing at Aylesbury's Friars Club at the Borough Assembly Hall, 1971. If ever there was something to put Aylesbury on the map, this club was surely it. It was started by David Stopps after a local schoolteacher, Robin Pike, suggested the idea. The first gig was held on 2 June 1969 at the New Friarage Hall in Walton Street, and featured Mandrake Paddle Steamer and Mike Cooper. (D.R. Stopps)

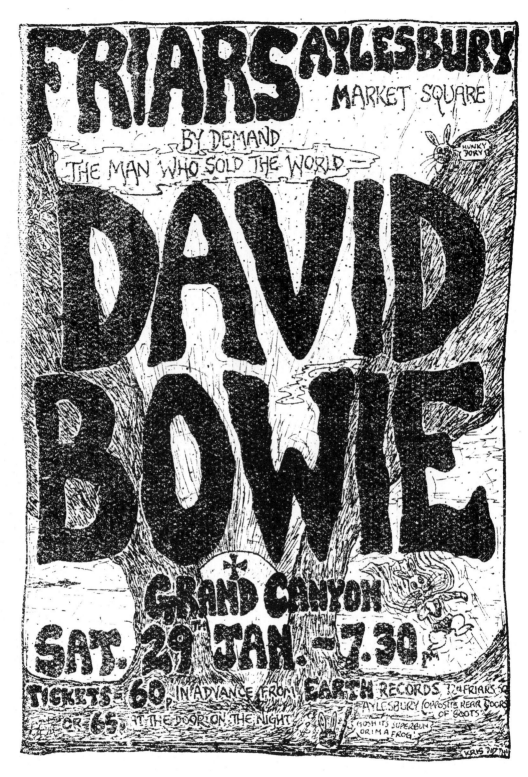

It's 1972 and David Bowie makes his second appearance at the Friars Club at the Borough Assembly Hall. He had his first concert here on 25 September 1971. Later that year he appeared along with other artists such as Lou Reed, Roxy Music, Genesis and Wizzard . . . the list goes on. Some of the foremost musicians of their day were featured at Friars, making it a legendary place to be. *(D.R. Stopps)*

Market day in Friars Square, 1973. The shop facing us to the left is Boots the Chemist. In 1983 they moved to their present site in Hale Leys Shopping Centre. *(R. Adams)*

Sports day at Elmhurst Infant School, 1973. On the day large rubber mats were provided for the children to sit on, and in the sunny summer weather they used to get very hot. Each class was labelled with different animals such as lions and elephants. *(K. Vaughan)*

Another view of Friars Square, 1973. Here we see the completed Woolworths section of the square stretching across the back with the County Offices towering behind it. The photograph also shows where the market ended up. It was here in Friars Square until 1991 when, during the square's modernization, it moved back to the Market Square. *(M. Sale)*

Looking down Buckingham Street, 1974. Page's the baker is seen on the right and further down the road is the large office block of Heron House. *(M. Sale)*

Children on the Quarrendon estate dressed up for the Queen's Silver Jubilee of 1977. *(R. Adams)*

Earlier in this book we've seen a couple of school photographs from the first quarter of the century. Here is one from Elmhurst Infant School in 1977. The teacher was Mr Norwood, and the boy with the zipped cardigan in the middle row later became an author of books about Aylesbury (including this one). *(K. Vaughan)*

David Stopps pictured with Phil Collins and Peter Gabriel on 24 August 1979 at the Friars Club. Peter was doing a concert at the time and Phil turned up unexpectedly to play African drums and congas. The photograph was taken by Armando Gallo. In 1970 Peter Gabriel broke his ankle at a Genesis concert here. During the show he leapt off the stage into the crowd hoping they would catch him. To his surprise they just parted and he fell to the floor. He was subsequently taken to the Royal Bucks Hospital. Genesis made a number of appearances at Aylesbury; their last gig was on 22 March 1980. The last concert at Friars was on 22 December 1984 and featured Marillion. Its closure was headlined in the *Bucks Herald* 'The Day the Music Died'. Will there be another Friars concert? You never know. . . *(D. Stopps)*

An advert for Earth Records in Friars Square. The shop was run by David Stopps and was the place to buy tickets for various Friars concerts. It was also a great place to get those hard to find records. *(R.J. Johnson)*

Baker's cycle and toy shop in Buckingham Street, 1979. Next to it Chamberlin's motor engineers site has been cleared in readiness for the construction of Sainsbury's supermarket. *(R. Adams)*

The 1980s to the End of the Century

Shops in Buckingham Street, June 1984, indicating the variety of fast food that we have all come to expect. *(R. Adams)*

FRIARS

Nº 934

PRESENTS LIVE ON STAGE
AN ORIGINAL FRIARS AYLESBURY LEGEND

GENESIS

TONY BANKS   PHIL COLLINS   MIKE RUTHERFORD

Saturday, 22nd March.   7.30 p.m.

MAXWELL HALL, MARKET SQ., AYLESBURY

This Ticket Value 350p (including VAT)

Friars Aylesbury is a Club and therefore it is essential that Membership Cards are produced on the night even if an advance ticket has been purchased. If you are not a member, membership must be obtained on the night. Minimum age for membership is 16 years. Life Membership is 25p (including VAT) Thank you.

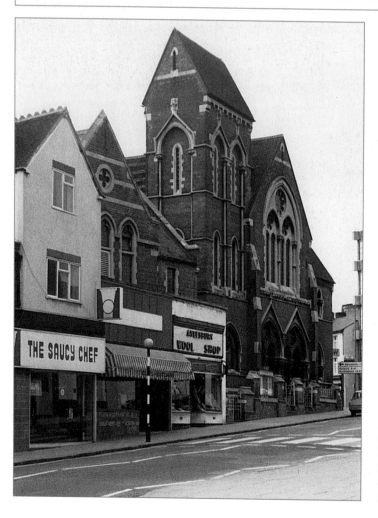

A ticket for the final concert that Genesis played at Friars on 22 March 1980. This was arguably the biggest gig ever held at the club. Tickets first went on sale on a cold Sunday morning in February. The queue for tickets started on the Friday and people were even camping in the cattle market, which just shows what a major event this was at the time. *(D.R. Stopps)*

High Street, 1980. Here we see the Congregational church pictured shortly before work started on its demolition for the construction of Hale Leys Shopping Centre. The main church tower was retained and integrated into the main structure of the centre. *(R. Adams)*

The main entrance to the Borough Assembly Hall, 1980. This hall was at the rear of the Green Man pub in Market Square. It was a legendary music venue for many years. An earlier structure on this site had housed the Market Theatre and, a little later, the Grosvenor roller skating rink which was popular through the 1950s and '60s. *(D. Bailey)*

Here we can see the full extent of the Borough Assembly Hall. This is viewed from the temporary car park that was left after the demolition of the Bull's Head Hotel. Hale Leys Shopping Centre would soon be started and this large hall was demolished in the development. All major music events had since moved to the new Civic Centre, which opened in 1975. *(D. Bailey)*

The factory of Agro Electrical in Buckingham Street, March 1980. This large Victorian building stood at the bottom of Granville Street and was originally built as a bakery. Later it became home to the printing firm of Hunt Barnard. Now an office block stands on the site. *(R. Adams)*

Some girls wandering through Vale Park, May 1980. Just behind the girl in the middle is the drinking fountain that was moved from Kingsbury in the 1920s and is seen earlier in the book. *(R. Adams)*

The United Counties bus depot, May 1980. This was opened in 1949 and was built on the site of a row of cottages in Granville Place. Just recently this whole area was cleared and some new apartments have been built. *(R. Adams)*

A view down Railway Street, May 1980. The houses seen here were originally built for railway workers. Aylesbury's first railway station used to stand at the end of this street, hence its name. It was subsequently moved to the High Street. It was demolished in the early 1960s when the track was taken up after its closure. At the end of the street is the Prince of Wales pub, which has also disappeared. *(R. Adams)*

One of the floats in the carnival of July 1980. These floats would parade through the town and finally end up at the Edinburgh Playing Fields on Churchill Avenue where there was a fair. *(R. Adams)*

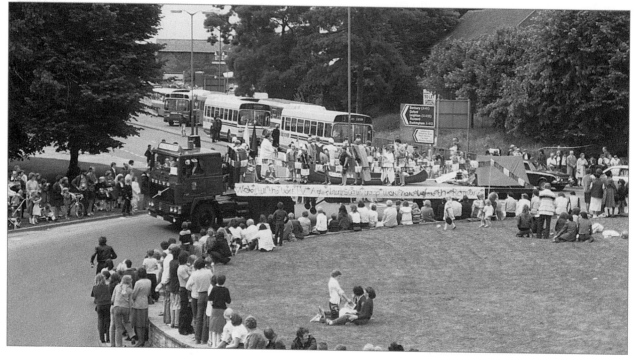

A carnival float going round the roundabout in Friarage Road, July 1980. *(R. Adams)*

A building at the bottom of Nelson Terrace and Whitehall Street, August 1980. Behind it was the builder's yard of George Adams. It was demolished in 1982. *(R. Adams)*

A view over the cattle market, May 1981. This was taken from the Civic Centre car park and beyond it are cranes used in the construction of a building which was to become known locally as the Blue Leanie. *(R. Adams)*

Another view from the Civic Centre car park, May 1981, this time looking towards the Vale Park with buildings at the rear of the White Hart and Chandos Hotel in Exchange in the foreground. *(R. Adams)*

A fire engine outside Browns in Buckingham Road, 1981. As well as selling lawnmowers, Browns were also sellers of agricultural machinery, which is seen on display to the right of the white barn. The car showrooms of Dutton Forshaw later took over this site, and it is now used as a forecourt. *(K. Vaughan)*

Pages of Aylesbury's bakery in Buckingham Street, May 1981. They closed in about 1984 and these buildings were demolished shortly after to be replaced by shops and offices. *(R. Adams)*

Halfords cycle shop in the High Street, September 1982. Next door is Hampdens bar and restaurant. Shortly after this photograph was taken, Halfords moved up the street to premises next to WH Smith. *(R. Adams)*

111

Mothercare in Friars Square, September 1982. This fronted Market Square and was one of the first shops to move here when the shopping centre opened in 1967. *(R. Adams)*

The Wimpy restaurant in Friars Square, 1983. The entrance was through some double doors which are seen on the left. They also led to the underground market. *(R. Adams)*

Another view of Friars Square, 1983. The Wimpy is seen again on the right and beyond is Woolworths, which occupied three floors and opened in 1969. It had a food hall on the ground floor, sweets, magazines and records on the first floor, and household items and a restaurant on the second floor. *(R. Adams)*

Looking up Buckingham Street, June 1984. Sainsbury's supermarket can be seen next to Baker's cycle and toy shop. At the very end of the street is the Harrow and Barleycorn pub. *(R. Adams)*

Buckingham Street, June 1984. The pub seen here had recently been refurbished. It was a combination of two pubs, the Harrow, and the Barleycorn, which was round the corner in Cambridge Street. To join the two a new entrance was built. The pub is now called the Farmyard and Firkin. *(R. Adams)*

The excavation in July 1985 of a piece of ground behind The Prebendal near St Mary's Church. The dig lasted through the summer and many different things were found there, including part of an Iron Age ditch that probably encircled the town at one time. Various ancient rubbish pits and building remains were also discovered. *(K. Vaughan)*

A view towards Friarage Road from the railway bridge, 21 May 1991. The road curving on the left is Station Way. The grass had recently been stripped from the area below and became a temporary car park for a short time while the new Safeway supermarket was being built. *(K. Vaughan)*

The refurbishment of Friars Square, 29 May 1991. The old Wimpy restaurant is seen here being demolished with the underground market below. This would later be covered over again. *(K. Vaughan)*

A view of the superstructure of the new Safeway supermarket, 27 July 1991. Friarage Road is in the foreground. *(K. Vaughan)*

Friars Square, 12 September 1991. Now that the old Wimpy has gone, work has begun on installing the concrete pillars to support the new steel floor. When complete, this area would be used for a handful of shops and a restaurant. *(K. Vaughan)*

116

While work was going on with the refurbishment of Friars Square I was able to take this photograph looking down Silver Street, 12 September 1991. It was a rare chance to see the whole length of the street again. Taken from Bourbon Street, this shows the Bell Hotel in Market Square appearing through the gap by the skip. This gap was eventually closed up again when the refurbishment was complete. (K. Vaughan)

The Bourbon Street entrance to Friars Square, 1 October 1991. A heavy duty drill is being used to demolish part of the structure. It certainly made the ground shudder when in use. (K. Vaughan)

Friars Square, 14 November 1991. Work has progressed a bit further now: a hole has been created for the installation of escalators, which would eventually lead down to the Cloisters shopping area. *(K. Vaughan)*

Friars Square viewed from the railway bridge, 15 February 1992. In the foreground work has begun on the new car park for the Safeway supermarket nearby. The crane on the horizon was erected in the middle of Friars Square to help in the construction of the new roof. *(K. Vaughan)*

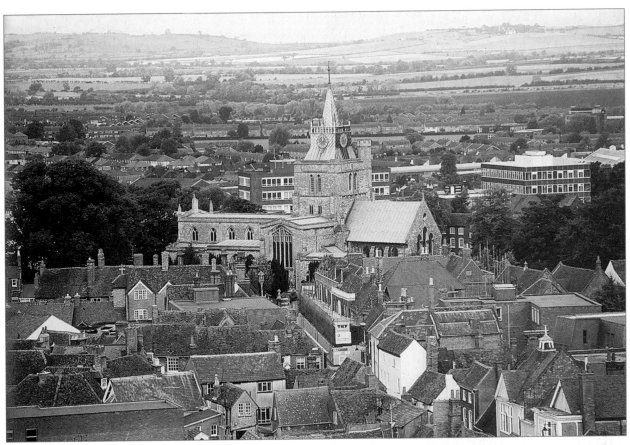

A view over the older part of town taken from the County Offices, 11 September 1993. In the centre is St Mary's Church, which still stands proud after 800 years. Surrounding it are the medieval streets and houses that form part of a conservation area. *(K. Vaughan)*

Hasberry's DIY shop in Temple Street, 1993. After serving the town for over fifty years, Hasberry's has now closed. *(K. Vaughan)*

The Dark Lantern in Silver Street, 1993. This pub remains as the only original building on that street. Others have been rebuilt and the rest has been obliterated by Friars Square. More recently the pub has had its name shortened to just the Lantern. *(K. Vaughan)*

A view of Station Street, 8 June 1997. The building seen here fronting Britannia Street together with the one behind it were demolished in May 2000 to make way for two large stores. Station Street itself also disappeared at that time. *(K. Vaughan)*

A view of Market Square from the County Offices, 9 May 1998. It is always interesting to see the town from this very tall building. At the top is a viewing area for the public that is usually accessible once a year. In this particular view the Bell Hotel is visible below, and in the distance is the dry ski slope at Watermead. (*K. Vaughan*)

Another view of the town, 12 June 1998. This was taken from the factory block of Nestlé and shows the Queen's Park estate below. At the very bottom are houses on the High Street. (*K. Vaughan*)

The car park on the site of the old cattle market, 2 August 1998. This was taken a day before work was to begin on the construction of the new cinema complex. *(K. Vaughan)*

Another view of the car park, 2 August 1998. Seen on the right is the old wall that stretches right down to Exchange Street. It used to be the boundary wall of the old White Hart Inn that stood in Market Square until 1864. To the rear of the inn were extensive grounds with orchards, gardens, a bowling green, kitchens and stables. *(K. Vaughan)*

The Odeon cinema in Cambridge Street, 27 October 1999. This photograph was taken shortly before its closure when the new cinema was built in Exchange Street. The building seen here still survives, although demolition is planned probably within a year. (*K. Vaughan*)

The new Hogshead pub, 19 December 1999. Next door to the left is another pub, Yates's Wine Lodge. These are both part of the cinema complex, which is seen on the next page. On the left are steps leading to the Civic Centre. (*K. Vaughan*)

The newly built ABC cinema viewed from Exchange Street, 19 December 1999. While it was being built I was expecting something more adventurous in design: it's a rather plain structure. Still, the cinema's pretty good inside! Its name has recently been changed to the Odeon. *(K. Vaughan)*

And so we reach the end of the century. A lot has changed in that period and many things still remain the same – like this view of Market Square taken on 19 December 1999 from the entrance to the King's Head, Aylesbury's oldest inn. Now the square has been pedestrianized it is comparatively safe to walk about without worrying too much about traffic, not unlike 100 years ago. The Market Square seemed the appropriate place to be on Millennium night. It was raining near midnight and there was a brief fireworks display. I stood there thinking of all the years that have passed, wondering what the people of the town were thinking when they stood there at the turn of the twentieth century. I wonder what changes the twenty-first century will see? *(K. Vaughan)*

Acknowledgements

I would like to thank the following people for their help and support during the compilation of this book. Richard J. Johnson for lending me some of his fine postcards and his insight into the history of the town. He also helped me find the amazing photographs of the Walton landmine damage which are deposited at the Record Office and form part of the Hazell, Watson & Viney scrapbook. Permission for their use was given by Mr Elliott Viney and I am very grateful. Also thanks to David Bailey for the use of his postcards and photographs. Also thanks to Peggy Sale for letting me use her fine photographs and postcards. I must also thank my uncle, Ron Adams, for digging out some useful photographs for the 1980s section – I would have been lost without them. Also John Millburn for the use of his fine photograph of his old auction rooms on page 68. To Douglas Joss for the loan of his fine aerial shot of Aylesbury in 1927 which appears on the front endpaper. To David Stopps for being so very helpful with information and memorabilia concerning the Friars Club of the 1970s and '80s. It made very interesting reading. And lastly to my family and friends for putting up with me during the six months that it took to compile this book.